Reasons To Be A Democrat

An Intelligent Guide

Max Hater

The most thoroughly researched and coherently argued supporter guide to date, "Reasons To Be A Democrat: An Intelligent Guide" is a supporter dissertation sure to provide vital data to help you make an educated party decision . Lawmakers require that we state the book is mostly blank and contains precisely 1600 words. In other 'words', it's a gag gift, but also a must-have addition to any supporter or hater's coffee table.

"Juuuuuust a bit outside!"

-Bob Uecker

www.MaxHater.com

Copyright © 2016 Max Hater, LLC

All rights reserved.

ISBN-13: 978-1546475323

ISBN-10: 154647532X

DEDICATION

This guide is dedicated to all the true supporters and haters out there. Without you, this book wouldn't be possible!

TABLE OF CONTENTS

1	Economics	Pg 5
2	Foreign Policy	Pg 17
3	Civil Rights	Pg 29
4	Education	Pg 41
5	Homeland Security	Pg 53
6	Energy	Pg 64
7	Jobs	Pg 74
8	Crime	Pg 86
9	Immigration	Pg 91
10	Values	Pg 101

1 ECONOMICS

Max Hater

Our analysis has found no reasons to be a supporter, based on Economics!

Our analysis has found no reasons to be a supporter, based on Economics!

Max Hater

Our analysis has found no reasons to be a supporter, based on Economics!

Our analysis has found no reasons to be a supporter, based on Economics!

Max Hater

Our analysis has found no reasons to be a supporter, based on Economics!

Reasons To Be A Democrat - An Intelligent Guide -

Our analysis has found no reasons to be a supporter, based on Economics!

Max Hater

Our analysis has found no reasons to be a supporter, based on Economics!

Our analysis has found no reasons to be a supporter, based on Economics!

Max Hater

Our analysis has found no reasons to be a supporter, based on Economics!

Our analysis has found no reasons to be a supporter, based on Economics!

Max Hater

Our analysis has found no reasons to be a supporter, based on Economics!

2 FOREIGN POLICY

Max Hater

Our analysis has found no reasons to be a supporter, based on Foreign Policy!

Our analysis has found no reasons to be a supporter, based on Foreign Policy!

Our analysis has found no reasons to be a supporter, based on Foreign Policy!

Our analysis has found no reasons to be a supporter, based on Foreign Policy!

Max Hater

Our analysis has found no reasons to be a supporter, based on Foreign Policy!

Our analysis has found no reasons to be a supporter, based on Foreign Policy!

Max Hater

Our analysis has found no reasons to be a supporter, based on Foreign Policy!

Our analysis has found no reasons to be a supporter, based on Foreign Policy!

Our analysis has found no reasons to be a supporter, based on Foreign Policy!

Our analysis has found no reasons to be a supporter, based on Foreign Policy!

Max Hater

Our analysis has found no reasons to be a supporter, based on Foreign Policy!

3 CIVIL RIGHTS

Max Hater

Our analysis has found no reasons to be a supporter, based on Civil Rights!

Our analysis has found no reasons to be a supporter, based on Civil Rights!

Max Hater

Our analysis has found no reasons to be a supporter, based on Civil Rights!

Our analysis has found no reasons to be a supporter, based on Civil Rights!

Max Hater

Our analysis has found no reasons to be a supporter, based on Civil Rights!

Reasons To Be A Democrat - An Intelligent Guide -

Our analysis has found no reasons to be a supporter, based on Civil Rights!

Max Hater

Our analysis has found no reasons to be a supporter, based on Civil Rights!

Our analysis has found no reasons to be a supporter, based on Civil Rights!

Max Hater

Our analysis has found no reasons to be a supporter, based on Civil Rights!

Our analysis has found no reasons to be a supporter, based on Civil Rights!

Max Hater

Our analysis has found no reasons to be a supporter, based on Civil Rights!

4 EDUCATION

Max Hater

Our analysis has found no reasons to be a supporter, based on Education!

Our analysis has found no reasons to be a supporter, based on Education!

Max Hater

Our analysis has found no reasons to be a supporter, based on Education!

Our analysis has found no reasons to be a supporter, based on Education!

Max Hater

Our analysis has found no reasons to be a supporter, based on Education!

Our analysis has found no reasons to be a supporter, based on Education!

Max Hater

Our analysis has found no reasons to be a supporter, based on Education!

Our analysis has found no reasons to be a supporter, based on Education!

Max Hater

Our analysis has found no reasons to be a supporter, based on Education!

Reasons To Be A Democrat - An Intelligent Guide -

Our analysis has found no reasons to be a supporter, based on Education!

Max Hater

Our analysis has found no reasons to be a supporter, based on Education!

5 HOMELAND SECURITY

Max Hater

Our analysis has found no reasons to be a supporter, based on Homeland Security!

Our analysis has found no reasons to be a supporter, based on Homeland Security!

Max Hater

Our analysis has found no reasons to be a supporter, based on Homeland Security!

Our analysis has found no reasons to be a supporter, based on Homeland Security!

Max Hater

Our analysis has found no reasons to be a supporter, based on Homeland Security!

Reasons To Be A Democrat - An Intelligent Guide -

Our analysis has found no reasons to be a supporter, based on Homeland Security!

Max Hater

Our analysis has found no reasons to be a supporter, based on Homeland Security!

Our analysis has found no reasons to be a supporter, based on Homeland Security!

Max Hater

Our analysis has found no reasons to be a supporter, based on Homeland Security!

Reasons To Be A Democrat - An Intelligent Guide -

Our analysis has found no reasons to be a supporter, based on Homeland Security!

6 ENERGY

Our analysis has found no reasons to be a supporter, based on Energy!

Our analysis has found no reasons to be a supporter, based on Energy!

Our analysis has found no reasons to be a supporter, based on Energy!

Our analysis has found no reasons to be a supporter, based on Energy!

Our analysis has found no reasons to be a supporter, based on Energy!

Max Hater

Our analysis has found no reasons to be a supporter, based on Energy!

Reasons To Be A Democrat - An Intelligent Guide -

Our analysis has found no reasons to be a supporter, based on Energy!

Our analysis has found no reasons to be a supporter, based on Energy!

Our analysis has found no reasons to be a supporter, based on Energy!

Max Hater

7 JOBS

Our analysis has found no reasons to be a supporter, based on Jobs!

Max Hater

Our analysis has found no reasons to be a supporter, based on Jobs!

Our analysis has found no reasons to be a supporter, based on Jobs!

Max Hater

Our analysis has found no reasons to be a supporter, based on Jobs!

Our analysis has found no reasons to be a supporter, based on Jobs!

Max Hater

Our analysis has found no reasons to be a supporter, based on Jobs!

Our analysis has found no reasons to be a supporter, based on Jobs!

Max Hater

Our analysis has found no reasons to be a supporter, based on Jobs!

Our analysis has found no reasons to be a supporter, based on Jobs!

Max Hater

Our analysis has found no reasons to be a supporter, based on Jobs!

Our analysis has found no reasons to be a supporter, based on Jobs!

Max Hater

8 CRIME

Our analysis has found no reasons to be a supporter, based on crime!

Max Hater

Our analysis has found no reasons to be a supporter, based on crime!

Reasons To Be A Democrat - An Intelligent Guide -

Our analysis has found no reasons to be a supporter, based on crime!

Our analysis has found no reasons to be a supporter, based on crime!

9 IMMIGRATION

Our analysis has found no reasons to be a supporter, based on immigration!

Our analysis has found no reasons to be a supporter, based on immigration!

Max Hater

Our analysis has found no reasons to be a supporter, based on immigration!

Our analysis has found no reasons to be a supporter, based on immigration!

Max Hater

Our analysis has found no reasons to be a supporter, based on immigration!

Reasons To Be A Democrat - An Intelligent Guide -

Our analysis has found no reasons to be a supporter, based on immigration!

Max Hater

Our analysis has found no reasons to be a supporter, based on immigration!

Our analysis has found no reasons to be a supporter, based on immigration!

Max Hater

Our analysis has found no reasons to be a supporter, based on immigration!

10 VALUES

Max Hater

Our analysis has found no reasons to be a supporter, based on values!

Our analysis has found no reasons to be a supporter, based on values!

Max Hater

Our analysis has found no reasons to be a supporter, based on values!

Our analysis has found no reasons to be a supporter, based on values!

ABOUT THE AUTHOR

Max Hater holds a B.S. (the alternative B.S. to a Bachelor of Science) in Hater and Supporter Analysis. Hater has accumulated years of thorough research and analysis of these supporters and haters. His unique work provides an understanding of the theories of supporter and hater behavior regarding a broad range of topics, as well as analysis of the empirical research on the emotions, thoughts, and behaviors of these supporters and haters. Using a multidisciplinary approach, a variety of fascinating topics such as identification, worship, and motivation have been identified and examined. This book provides an understanding of the importance of these supporters and haters and provides an intelligent guide for following the same motives to become the best supporter and/or hater possible.

Find Max on Twitter: @MaxHater1
Find Max on Facebook: @MaxHater1
Find Max on Instagram: @MaxHater

www.MaxHater.com

CPSIA information can be obtained
at www.ICGtesting.com
Printed in the USA
LVOW10s2314110617
537764LV00008B/388/P